Garden Mediations
Refreshing Moments with God

By Kimberly Dawn Rempel

Garden Mediations By Kimberly Dawn Rempel

Published © 2017 By Kimberly Dawn Rempel

All rights reserved. No portion of this book may be reproduced in any form without permission from the Author/Publisher.

TABLE OF CONTENTS

Introduction 6
Day 1: We Sow, God Grows 7
Day 2: The Secret that Birch Trees Know 9
Day 3: Fruit in our Weakness 11
Day 4: Sowing Seeds on Gravel 13
Day 5: Dawn Breaks Slowly 15
Day 6: When Weeds Overwhelm 17
Day 7: The Practical Value of Beauty 19
Day 8: The Promise of Newness 21
Day 9: The Measure of Tomatoes 23
Day 10: Glimpsing God on the Sun-Dappled Path 25
Day 11: When You Don't Know What to Pray 27
Day 12: I'm a Potato and So Are You 29
Day 13: Treasure and Applause for this Day 31
Day 14: There Will Always Be Weeds 33
Day 15: Love Struck 35
Day 16: Look Up 37
17: Defying Soul Gravity 39
18: The Sunday Morning Tulip Miracle 41
19: Finding One True Thing 43

20: Growth When Transplanted..45

21: On Maple Sap and Human Effort..47

22: His Mercies Are Surprising Every Morning 50

23: Faith in the Fog...52

24: Fruit in All Seasons 55

25: When it Feels Like Nothing I Do Makes a Difference 58

About the Author 60

INTRODUCTION

Welcome to my garden. I'm so glad you've come.

Our small acreage nestled in the country has been our home for over a decade. Tall, mature Maple trees surround the little house, shading the deck, and providing us with sap each year. Much has been harvested from the gardens here – rest, frustration, lessons in faith, escape from the house, and many flowers and vegetables too.

Some of my best moments with God have been spent witnessing the sunrise, eagerly awaiting the unfurling of spring's first tulips, and trimming back tomato plants, remembering Jesus' words about vines and branches.

I've been privately enjoying reading and rereading these meditations for a few years, becoming encouraged and refreshed time and again. I'm so glad I wrote them. But it occurred to me that I should really share them with you so you could be blessed and encouraged too.

Got your coffee? Comfy in your patch of sun? Let's dig in.

DAY 1: WE SOW, GOD GROWS

Every year when I start a garden, it ends up being a weird exercise in faith.

I rummage through my stash of seeds, and wonder if they're too old to be any good. Maybe I stored them improperly and they're ruined.

Still, I plant them and wrestle with believing they'll grow. Every day I check on the seeds, wondering if the soil is too dry, too wet, or maybe contains some kind of seed-killing bacteria.

Then, to my surprise, the seedlings burst up through the soil, and I'm excited… for a day. Then I return to worrying they'll die because of wind or lack of sunlight, or maybe I'll water them too much or not enough. Even when they're full grown, I doubt their fruit will ripen in time.

Every year I doubt the process and every year I'm surprised when the plants live and yield produce.

When I told a friend this, she challenged me to celebrate the sowing instead of worrying. Sowing is our part and the growth of those seeds is God's job.

I've struggled a lot with expectations and the disappointment that comes when I don't get the results I think I should. This happens in ministry, marriage, parenting, friendship, and writing. When I invest myself in something, I do it with a goal in mind. I expect results. Whether that means receiving more attention in relationships, or having well-behaved, God-loving children, or watching people grow spiritually because of my investment, I expect it.

The thing is though, that every one of those outcomes is completely out of my hands. I can't make my children love and serve God, and I can't make people grow spiritually. All I can do is sow the seeds God gives me to sow; the growth of those seeds is his job.

This year, I will plant and water seeds with a renewed mind. I will reject doubt and worry and instead unfurl my hands and release my expectations to God. The whole process and all the provision of sun and wind and rain comes from Him. I can't grow a single tomato. All I can do is sow the seed and tend the garden. The growth and fruit all comes from Him.

There's a fine line between the hopeful, trusting expectation that God will produce fruit in my life or someone else's, and the expectation that when I do 'x', I deserve the result of 'y'. The critical difference is who I rely on.

This year, I will practice letting go of my need for results. Whether it's growing tomatoes or wanting someone to know Jesus more, I will sow the seeds and tend the garden, but I will work at not being disappointed when nothing appears to be happening. Instead I will trust that something absolutely is happening.

This is faith; to trust beyond sight.

> *"Faith is the confidence that what we hope for will actually happen; it gives us assurance about things we cannot see"*
>
> Hebrews 11:1

Response:

In what area of your life to you ache for results? Parenting? Work? Relationships? Tell God about the results you ache for. Then practice trusting Him beyond what you want, believing that His plan is best.

DAY 2: THE SECRET THAT BIRCH TREES KNOW

Poplars are my favorite tree.

They always seem like they're celebrating.

Round leaves dangle like earrings. Sunlight glints off of their smooth sides as they gently dangle in a breeze.

When the wind pushes past, thousands of leaves wiggle, bringing the tree to life in a swarm of flapping butterflies.

Best of all is the sound of a million tiny leaves brushing together in the wind. Sometimes it sounds like ocean waves. Sometimes it sounds like it looks – like a thousand round leaves applauding.

A forest of trees stands in ovation for the One who made today.

And we have the honor of watching.

Of joining in.

Of awaiting the encore.

> *"Let the heavens be glad, and the earth rejoice!*
>
> *Let the sea and everything in it shout his praise!*
>
> *Let the fields and their crops burst out with joy!*
>
> *Let the trees of the forest sing for joy*
>
> *before the Lord, for he is coming!"*
>
> Psalm 96:11-13a

Response:

Today is just about discovering some awe of God. Consider an aspect of creation and reflect on how our majestic God took time to shape those details. Even the inside of a flower has unique shapes and colors, some never to be seen by human eyes. Still, it glorifies Him. Soak in awe of our wonderful God, and let His majesty move you to praise.

DAY 3: FRUIT IN OUR WEAKNESS

Every year, tiny white caps emerge from crevices in our old Maple trees.

I admire their intricate design and tenacity to grow in dark places, but they also make me a little sad. I know our Maples are slowly dying. These mushrooms prove it. And every year there seem to be more. Despite their age and weakening though, these Maples are bearing fruit even as they die.

Mushrooms are the fruit from the internal infection of spores. What is inside is simply coming out. Likewise, our faith in difficult times is the evidence of things unseen. It's evidence to others that we are followers of Jesus, and that he is real and able and powerful in our lives.

It reminds me of God's baffling promise that His strength is made perfect in weakness. Some fruit, maturity, and holiness can actually not be understood or experienced without weakness and death.

I think of my mom as an example of this. It was only during her battle with cancer that her faith became more obvious. As her suffering deepened, so did her faith. More and more conversations were centered on faith in Jesus. People had told me she was a woman of strong faith, but I didn't actually know it. Faith talk was reserved for well-timed one-on-one conversations, and those didn't happen very often. Until cancer. Suddenly the one-hour commutes to appointments and treatments and all the hours in waiting rooms afforded us much time to talk and reflect together. Cancer also necessitated the fierce pursuit of things to be thankful for. And she was good at it.

In her final years, I got to know my mom as the strong woman of faith others saw her as. I'm so deeply thankful! I'm also aware it might not have happened without the hours and perspective that Cancer lent.

It's hard to see and harder to believe when we're suffering, but, even in our weakness and dying, God produces fruit in our lives. (Gal 5:22)

Faith is the confidence that what we hope for will actually happen; it gives us assurance about things we cannot see.

Hebrews 11:1

Response:

Think of a time of weakness in your life. What good can you see came from it? Maybe you're currently in a time of weakness and can't see that fruit yet. Ask God to show you some good He's working through this circumstance. Thank Him for it, and trust that more is coming. He is able to do far more than we can hope or imagine.

DAY 4: SOWING SEEDS ON GRAVEL

The sun blazed as I worked in the yard. The children played on a play structure nearby. Soon, our two red-faced children fled from the structure and dashed to a shady corner. I wiped sweat from my brow and went to the house to get us all some cool drinks. They sipped water eagerly as we sat clustered in a patch of shade.

Just then, a starry fluff of tree-seed found us. It meandered in the humid air, landing on a shoulder. The little boy picked it off and flung it away. The seed wafted lower, inches above driveway stones. The future didn't look too promising for the little seed...

Have you ever felt like you're sowing seeds on gravel? Like your efforts are invisible, or worse, fruitless? When we pray for loved ones to turn to Jesus or try to teach our kids right from wrong, these seeds seem hard to sow and take forever to grow. It's tiring to invest ourselves, and, when we do not see fruit from our efforts, we become discouraged or tempted to give up. So how can we fend off this discouragement?

In our lowest moments, when we wonder what the point of all this learning and growing and effort is, God's Word comforts us:

> *"My child, don't make light of the Lord's discipline, and don't give up when He corrects you..."*
>
> Hebrews 12:5

I love that. He *knows* we are tempted to give up. All this growing in the faith and training for heavenly living (which is what discipline is) is hard, and He knows it.

> *"... But God's discipline is always good for us, so that we might share in His holiness. No discipline is enjoyable while it is happening –it's painful! But afterward there will be a peaceful harvest of right living for those who are trained in this way."*
>
> Hebrews 12:10

This passage confirms the hope we have – that all the striving and effort to grow in faith and serve Him well, whether we see the fruit or not, will, guaranteed, yield "a peaceful harvest of right living". At the very least, the fruit we can expect is that we are being trained in God's ways.

If you feel like you're sowing seeds on gravel, take comfort in Galatians 5:22, "... the Holy Spirit produces this kind of fruit in our lives..." It is *God's* work in our hearts that grows anything. It is not the quantity or location of our sowing that produces fruit. Even Jesus' miracles and healings did not convert all who saw or received. His own disciple, Judas, did not believe! Jesus left the results to God, the One who works in hearts. How much more should we?

The results are not ours. Continuing to sow in obedience though, is definitely ours to do. And we will be rewarded for it. (Gal 5:22, Gal 6: 9, 10, Eph 1, Matt 6:4, 8, Luke 19:17)

What does it look like practically? It looks like a tree releasing thousands of seeds to the wind, year after year. It looks like loving people whether it's easy or hard, and remembering, always remembering, that we are not responsible for the results. That's God's job. Ours is simply to obey.

If we can let go of our desire to point to *what we did* as proof of the worth of our efforts, and instead point to *who He is* as proof of the worth of our efforts, we will walk in peace and strength, wherever the wind blows our seeds.

Response: Thank God for the seeds He's given you to plant and that He is in control of the results. Ask Him to let go of your desire for results and to strengthen your trust in His ability to take care of what you've sown.

DAY 5: DAWN BREAKS SLOWLY

I love sitting on my deck with a cup of steaming coffee to watch the sunrise. It's a spectacular sight to witness majestic pinks edge morning clouds and opulent orange and purple splash across the sky. But all that's not even the best part.

The glory of the morning is in its slow coming.

Can you imagine if it happened instantly? The sun would pop straight up from the horizon, resting in some appropriate 'it's now officially morning' spot and we'd miss the color and splendor of its colorful arrival.

As I sip coffee and watch, I can't tell in that slow emergence of the sun at what point dawn ends and day begins. It made me think of all the spiritual dark times I'd come out of. My emergence from those times seemed way too slow to me, and I could never point to an exact moment when the trial was over.

In times of doubt or fear or general spiritual wrestling, we pray fervently for relief; instant relief. But it rarely comes as a sudden flash of light. Most of the time it seems slow; painfully slow. And, when we're in it, the slowness of it can make the dark seem deeper. In the waiting, the doubts seem more convincing. In the desperation, the fears can chill us to the core. Yet, slowly, the darkness fades and somehow we end up in the light.

Once arrived on the other side of the trial, we are hard pressed to point to how we overcame it. Like dawn breaking, we don't know quite when dark became light.

This is a common exit from spiritually dark times, and it can be frustrating. All we want is for it to be high noon already, with the unmistakable sun shining obviously in the clear sky. But it's a slow process. Growth often is.

As we wait for dawn to break, we learn to trust that yes, after every darkness the light does come. And yes, it comes slowly, quietly, and in a way that's difficult to pinpoint, but it is surely happening. And yes, when we wait on the Lord, he is faithful, every time. In the waiting, we learn trust and maybe even develop a joyful anticipation of the dawn we learn it does come.

I hope that as I grow in Christ, my struggle to trust morphs into a contented anticipation for the "joy set before me". I pray that my faith will grow, yielding the ability to sit still and quiet even in the long dark night. I want to live always confident that dawn is on its way in His perfect time.

"Now faith is confidence in what we hope for and assurance about what we do not see."

Hebrews 11:1

Response:

Think of a time when you were waiting for light to dawn in your darkness. Thank God that the dawn did break that time, and that it will come again. Ask Him to grow you in the ability to sit still and quiet even in the long, dark night, trusting Him both in the dark times and in the light.

DAY 6: WHEN WEEDS OVERWHELM

Weeks of rain had stunted the cauliflower and kale. Spinach, planted in the lowest spot in the garden, had not come up at all. The tomato plants seemed to be rotting. Every manner of weeds though, appeared to flourish.

With garden hoe in hand, I prepared to beat back countless weeds. As soon as I saw grass had again advanced through the fence and reclaimed six inches of the garden's border, I realized it was beyond hoeing. This would be a hands-and-knees effort.

I assumed the position and uprooted the offending grass to defend my meagre crop. The grass stood tall and strong, staunchly resisting my efforts. Nearby cauliflower and corn, by comparison, appeared weak and small, showing no promise of fruit by mid-July. The harvest did not look promising. After a while my wrists ached and I had barely covered four feet of fence. Hopelessness started to weigh. *What is the point of defending such a small harvest? How wise is this as an investment of my time?* I considered tilling everything under...

Sometimes it seems like this is the state of the world, doesn't it? The powers of evil relentlessly advance to reclaim borders and choke out the harvest. At times, when evil seems overwhelming, our hope for the harvest may falter. But, even in a state of overwhelm, we are not alone. We have a great tool at our disposal to fend off discouragement and revive hope; that tool is praise.

> "Why am I discouraged? Why is my heart so sad? I will put my hope in God! I will praise him again- my Savior and my God!"
>
> Psalm 42:11

David recognized the power of praise to fend off discouragement. Something powerful happens when we take our eyes off of ourselves or our troubles and look instead on the One who has overcome and who gives us the victory.

*And let us run with endurance the race God has set before us.
We do this by keeping our eyes on Jesus, the champion who initiates and perfects our faith.*

Hebrews 12:1b,2a

Let's not give up. As we continue to fix our eyes on Him, he will produce a harvest in and through us.

*"You will always harvest what you plant. Those who live only to satisfy their own sinful nature will harvest decay and death from that sinful nature. But those who live to please the Spirit will harvest everlasting life from the Spirit. So let's not get tired of doing what is good.
At just the right time we will reap a harvest of blessing if we don't give up.*

(Galatians 6:7-9)

Response:

Thank God for the people he has placed in your life to protect you and help you grow in Him. Thank Him for the promise that we "will always harvest what we plant" and "at just the right time we will reap a harvest of blessing if we don't give up". Ask Him for the endurance and courage to not give up sowing for Him.

DAY 7: THE PRACTICAL VALUE OF BEAUTY

I've always valued practicality over aesthetics. Things like home décor, vehicle polish, and jewellery all held little value for me. To me, beauty was impractical; an unnecessary extra. As a result, my house is not ornate, furnishings and clothing are simple, and vacations, well, what is that?

When I discussed this one day with my equally utilitarian friend, she told me of her experience gardening with her mom many years ago.

One day, as a young girl tending the vegetable garden with her mom, she noticed her mom planted beautiful flowers of varied colors and species right there among the oh-so-practical potatoes.

"Why do you plant flowers here?" she'd asked.

"To attract the bees, so they'll pollinate the vegetables," her mom had said.

As she recounted the story, we both considered the value – the practicality - of beauty. If I'd thought about it, I supposed I knew. Every time I look up at the blue sky and sighed, I knew the power of beauty to restore the soul.

Our wonder of the beauty of creation, of God, refreshes our souls.

The times I have felt most refreshed have been those moments I was captivated by beauty and restored to a posture of praise and thanks. The tasks, lists, and goals that normally filled my head would fall away, and I was suddenly allowed to just be. More than that, in that moment I remember that there is way more to life than just me.

When I'm focused on tasks and goals, it's all about me - what I decide, what I can accomplish, and what I need. Awe though, is all about Someone else who is grander, more able, and more important than me. The Creator of shooting stars and ocean waves endlessly inspires wonder, refreshing our souls with His beauty.

It's in that place of reverence I am truly refreshed – jolted out of lists and tasks and invited to have a seat and behold something bigger. Like having a seat at the symphony, I smile and watch the show, amused, bewildered, and completely satisfied.

Response:

Take a few minutes today to sit in awe of God's masterful skill. Think about how He swirls clouds, breathes wind across the grass, and moves light. As you consider His power and wisdom and attention to detail, let awe of His beauty satisfy and refresh you.

DAY 8: THE PROMISE OF NEWNESS

It was June. I sat on the deck, panning our thick grass and greening garden. It had been a long year and a half of wrestling with a life-changing decision. One of the hardest choices I ever wrestled with was whether or not to leave a church family we'd been part of for a decade.

We'd grown so much there, raised our children there, and discovered dear friends who were precious to us. We didn't want to leave and yet, somehow, we felt like our time there was over. The sweet trills of birds went unnoticed that morning as the tireless limbo weighed heavy on my heart. Oh, how I ached for resolution, for clarity.

With pen in hand, I traced the handle of a coffee mug. "Holy Spirit, what do you have to say to me today?" The pen was poised to record what I'd otherwise forget. I scrawled the words.

… *coming soon* …

"What's coming soon Lord?"

… *newness* …   The word was palpable. It swelled with feeling, like a seedling under soil not yet having touched light. And finally it burst through, bent, and unfurled stretching for the sun.

I leaned forward and licked parted lips. "When Lord?"

… *four* …

"Four days? Four Weeks?" I sprinkled questions about what would happen in the next four days, but heard nothing. Until finally,

… *you'll see*…

It felt like an unfinished flowerbed, tilled and half-planted. It was hard to leave it there like that, but the gardener had moved on. He would return when the time was right. He does it all the time. The wait was hard, but I love discovering the flowers and greenery he adds quietly when I'm not looking. So I wandered the proverbial garden, admiring his work while I waited.

Months passed; hard months of struggle and aching. I felt wrapped in a straight jacket – restricted and pressed down. With arms tied, still stuck in that awful limbo, I continued to wander, remembering the past work he'd done and allowing them to give me hope.

Finally, I suddenly felt release. The decision could now be made, We were clearly released and led to our new church home. The limbo could end. Ah, my mouth turned up and I remembered how to smile again.

Deeply relieved, I reflected one day beneath the trees overlooking the garden. As I remembered the feeling of that unfinished garden God had tilled and half-planted, I recalled the promise of newness. Suddenly I realized the promise was made four months before. Now, the time for newness had come, and it felt just like He said it would. That patch of garden was complete.

And He knew - what would happen, how I would respond, even when I would remember the promise again – He knew it all. More than that, He planned it.

I don't know why he makes us wait or how He knows how we'll respond. But if you'd ask Him, I can imagine what the Gardener might say.

'you'll see…'

"For I know the plans I have for you," says the Lord, "They are plans for good and not for disaster, to give you a future and a hope. In those days when you pray, I will listen. If you look for me wholeheartedly, you will find me."

Jeremiah 29:11-13

Response:

Whatever you're facing, whether a time of pain or relief, make time today to deliberately remember all the times God was there for you, rescued you, or brought newness. Thank Him for His plan, and let it build your faith and hope for the newness He has in store for you.

DAY 9: THE MEASURE OF TOMATOES

The tomato plants had grown well over three feet tall. I couldn't see any fruit through the jungle of greenery. There were hundreds of promising, pretty flowers, but it was too late in the season for them to become anything. Winter neared and there was no time.

Kneeling with scissors, I examined each stem, each branch. All fruitless branches were removed and tossed on a heap. Hundreds of flowers - beautiful, full-of-promise, look-just-like-they-should flowers, had to be sacrificed for the good of the fruit.

I clipped fruitless yellow. If allowed to stay, these flowers and extra branches would continue to drain energy from the plant. Tomatoes wouldn't grow or mature, and the flowers would continue to bloom and promise, but yield nothing.

Quickly and ruthlessly, I clipped stems and branches. Thick ones. All the effort and time and energy that went into growing those precious stem didn't matter. It was not producing fruit, and that had to be the measure.

That was the measure.

Jesus is the vine, and we are the branches ...so which branch am I? Or my church? Are we flower-filled, full of promise but yielding nothing? Are we producing immature fruit that will die for the sake of flowers? Or have we found fruit and nourished it for a great harvest?

Therefore, since we are surrounded by such a huge crowd of witnesses to the life of faith, let us strip off every weight that slows us down, especially the sin that so easily trips us up. And let us run with endurance the race God has set before us. We do this by keeping our eyes on Jesus, the champion who initiates and perfects our faith.

Hebrews 12:1-3a (NLT)

Response:

Ask God to reveal to you the fruit He's producing in your life. It might look like growth in character or the fruit of the Spirit (Gal 5), or it might look like the provision of opportunities or relationships. Thank Him for the work He's already begun in you.

Ask God to reveal a weight that slows you down and impedes the growth of these fruits in your life. Commit to stripping that weight so you can run with endurance the race set before you.

DAY 10: GLIMPSING GOD ON THE SUN-DAPPLED PATH

The grassy path wound through Poplars, trodden to dirt in places. I paced briskly, focused on the goal in mind. As I made my way quickly on my way somewhere, my eyes remained on the grass and dirt beneath me, keeping watch for mud patches as I sped through. Suddenly I realized I was missing the point.

Surrounded by beauty, I chose to focus on mud. I could have been relaxing in nature, enjoying its beauty, but instead paced briskly through it.

I slowed, raising my eyes to the woods. Flecks of sunlight wiggled under tree tops. I slowed a little more, and noticed an empty spider web. I stop moving; decidedly watching whatever stillness would allow me to see. A statue in the woods, I waited. Poison Ivy shimmied in patches above crunching noises. I pretended to be a tree as the scampering neared.

A tiny chipmunk leaped from under tall ivy onto a fallen Poplar. Spotting me, he stilled.

Perched and standing, we stared at each other, unmoving.

In the pause, the blur of swaying green suddenly became a collection of intricate details along a sun-speckled path. Dewy webs tenuously hung. The cautious chipmunk that now munched an acorn, eyed me, unblinking. Round leaves flapped. Pointed leaves fanned humid air.

Suddenly I realized all the world was a dappled path. Each moment, each person, is an intricate detail in God's secret design. Perhaps, in the pausing, one even glimpses God himself. Perhaps He hides in this secret garden, visible only when we still to look.

Response:

Decide to still yourself today, even if just for a few minutes, to focus on the intricate details of creation. Sit in a place surrounded by nature and silently absorb it. Listen for sounds. Watch for its movements. Remember those 3D pictures that only revealed their hidden image when stared at in a certain way? That. Do that. When you begin to see the intricate details come alive, thank God for His attention to detail, and for the refreshment of stillness and awe.

DAY 11: WHEN YOU DON'T KNOW WHAT TO PRAY

As I hunched to pick weeds from cracked, hard soil, I remembered the prayer requests scrawled on a paper in the house. I tossed roots and leaves onto grass as I began to pray.

"Lord... would you please..." I sighed, bent over weeds. The prayer left unsaid, I was already bored. *God, I said all this already. I asked you already. Do I really need to ask again? At what point do I become a Pharisee babbling?*

How does one 'continue to pray' for others? How many times must a person bring their requests to God? Surely He's not as forgetful as I am...?

Sometimes I don't know what to pray for, or what more to say because I feel I've said it all. That's when I take comfort in God's promise to help us even with prayer.

"And the Holy Spirit helps us in our weakness. For example, we don't know what God wants us to pray for. But the Holy Spirit prays for us with groanings that cannot be expressed in words. And the Father who knows all hearts knows what the Spirit is saying, for
the Spirit pleads for us believers in harmony with God's own will."

Romans 8:26, 27

Sometimes it's hard to know how to pray for ourselves or others. Should we pray for healing from an illness or for the release of death? Should we pray someone gets that job or that they don't get it because God's plan is something better?

We don't know. But God does. And He hears the heart behind our prayer, and the Holy Spirit in us pleads for us in harmony with God's will. Amazing.

Response:

Thank God for allowing you to become bored or confused about your prayers because it makes you dependant on Him. Ask Him what to pray and, if you're still not sure, praise Him and ask with confidence that His will – His best plan – will be worked out for the good of those who love Him.

DAY 12: I'M A POTATO AND SO ARE YOU

The children and I had dug rows and were ready to plan potatoes. As I cupped a firm red potato in hand, I thoughtfully ran a thumb across its eye tops. It was alive, yet dying. There was a parallel there....

We pressed potato pieces into the long, narrow graves. My daughter's tiny fingers carefully placed each one, eyes-up. I clutch the garden hoe and stood above the line of potato pieces stretched out before me. The metal blade scraped and dirt tumbled over each piece and I wondered what it looked like in there, beneath the dirt, where life and death meet.

It probably looks a lot like you and me and doing life on earth. Both dying and alive, we were put in this place where pain and sorrow and struggles somehow help transform death to life.

Once we finished sowing the garden, the children and I walked across the yard to return tools to the shed. I turned back to glance the garden. It was full of manure, the cat was crouching to add more.

And all the transformation, that apparently needs heaps of manure and stink and bugs and dirt to accomplish that magic of change, happens where we can't see it.

And after each clump of eye tops dies to live, the grave will be opened and the fruit counted.

Then we will celebrate the fruit,
the process,
and the One who makes the magic happen
(and in the grave of all places).

It's all so ... God. He's brilliant like that.

But the Holy Spirit produces this kind of fruit in our lives: love, joy, peace, patience, kindness, goodness, faithfulness, [23] *gentleness, and self-control. There is no law against these things!*

Galatians 5:22,23a

For God is working in you, giving you the desire and the power to do what pleases him.

Philippians 2:13

Response:

Whatever season you're in, whether you feel spiritually dead or vibrant and alive, trust God's process of bringing life and producing fruit. Thank Him for the fruit He has produced in your life so far, and praise Him for His promise and ability to produce fruit in and through you.

DAY 13: TREASURE AND APPLAUSE FOR THIS DAY

Armed with a wooden stake, my daughter marched across our yard and etched Xs everywhere. Her older brother followed close behind, wielding his mini garden claw.

"HaHA!! 'X' marks the spot!!" he bellowed, and scratched furiously at the X she had marked. They marched around the yard that way in the hope of discovering bones.

From my cozy perch under a Willow tree, I admired how their random expedition is hopeful, yet without expectation. They never once asked if a treasure hunt would fit within their life purpose or if it contained enough meaning or served a goal. They just did it.

Is that allowed? Can I just ... be?

I perched on a bent Willow bough, and allowed stillness to open my ears.

The wind rushed through the trees, sounding like ocean waves.

Last year's leaves flapped on flat grass; a ceaseless applause for this day.

Can it be so simple? Am I allowed to just be, and not constantly measure the value of my every action or motive? Can I simply enjoy the day and give Him applause?

As I continued to watch my treasures seek treasures, and observe even creation itself bursting into praise and applause, I unearthed a treasure of my own. It is absolutely worthwhile and desirable to simply rejoice in the day God has made and to simply be glad in it. Let there be applause for this day.

"Shout to the LORD, all the earth;
break out in praise and sing for joy!"

Psalm 98:4

*"This is the day the LORD has made.
We will rejoice and be glad in it."*

Psalm 118:24

Response:

Spend some time rejoicing in the day, ideally out in nature. There's no right or wrong way to do this, either. Whether you're jogging, swimming, playing with the kids, weeding the garden, or sipping a latte on the patio, break into praise and sing for joy!

DAY 14: THERE WILL ALWAYS BE WEEDS

The speed with which weeds grow amazes me. They're everywhere, too! In the garden, the yard, even under the deck and between sidewalk tiles. Just when I think I've weeded all the beds, mowed all the grass, and edged all the edges, there they are, popping up all over. Again.

I know I shouldn't be surprised or even frustrated. There will always be weeds. My expectation that there ought not to be is unrealistic. One day, when I bent to pull them out again, the spiritual parallel hit me – I have a similar unrealistic expectation about holiness.

I expect to be able to pull the weeds of sin from my life and have them be gone forever. I expect, at some point, to be done. After walking with Jesus, learning many things, and growing in obedience, it's a little maddening to realize that I'm still all fleshy on the inside.

"You mean I'm not holy yet?!"

Here's the good news though. *I* may be shocked and appalled by my sin, but God saw it the whole time. He knows I'm all fleshy on the inside and still chooses to answer prayer, speak to my heart, and use and bless me every day. Me. The selfish, dirty, gross-on-the-inside human.

He's the One doing the revealing. I'm the one getting my eyes opened.

The best part is that He is not rejecting or condemning me either. He's not shaking His head in disappointment, I'm the one doing that. Growth takes time and He is patient. And, as long as I'm alive, there will always be weeds. Thankfully, Jesus is glad to join me to help pull them. Even when they grow back.

"And have you forgotten the encouraging words

God spoke to you as his children? He said,
"My child, don't make light of the Lord's discipline,
and don't give up when he corrects you.
For the Lord disciplines those he loves,
and he punishes each one he accepts as his child."

Hebrews 12:5,6

"So now there is no condemnation
for those who belong to Christ Jesus."

Romans 8:1

Response:

Thank the Lord for the assurance of His love and for His continued guidance and help. He is a good Father who weeds in the garden beside us, and is happy to. He is not harsh with us, but compassionate, merciful, and slow to anger.

DAY 15: LOVE STRUCK

Have you ever been awestruck by God's love for you? Maybe His Word suddenly came alive and you had a new, deeper understanding in that moment. Or maybe something someone said hit you like a surge of electricity, and God spoke a truth straight to your heart in that moment.

Those are precious moments when they happen, and excellent faith-builders to reflect on.

One such moment came for me one day as I stood outside on the deck, overlooking the yard and flower garden, contemplating God's love. While I was there, the wind picked up and I watched a storm brew nearby. It was coming fast.

Grey clouds swelled, climbing, almost racing, for the top of the sky. Air dampened all around me as heavy clouds edged closer. From my spot on the deck I saw one long cloud sprawled across the sky, its deep blue underbelly pregnant with rain. The far clouds rumbled. At the other end of the sky, rolling thunder followed a white flash. Then another. Two ends of sky stretched toward each other, competing to veil the sky. I could hardly believe it was happening, but they headed toward collision right above me.

I was honored to receive a front row seat to the rumbling convergence. As I watched, two skies become one thundering mass above me I felt like I was getting a private, personal glimpse of my heavenly Dad. It felt almost scandalous to even think such a thing – I'm not so special. Surely He has more important things to do and consider, more important people to invest in.

Converged clouds rumbled overhead, long and low and I couldn't stop grinning. God bent over fields in grey and flexed thunder muscles across the sky. Awed, I let a sigh escape as I drank in humid grey. He flexed again and winked lightening. Tree tops swayed, leaves quivered. Deep blue gave way to wash out grey. Like crystals sprinkling, it came - a gem curtain swept through the Poplar forest headed straight for me. Air thickened and gems fell louder, sweeping closer. I raised hands to sky, accepting the gift of that moment. Crystal orbs wet my outstretched hands. I laughed, courted and won by the strength of a God who bends and who winks from behind clouds with lightening.

Taste and see that the LORD IS GOOD. OH, THE JOYS OF THOSE WHO TAKE REFUGE IN HIM!

PSALM 34:8

Response:

God is not a distant, uninvolved being. He is alive and active, the functional Lord of our lives, and caring Father to His children. Do you believe that? If so, thank Him for his unabashed love and enjoyment of you. If not, are you willing to consider the possibility? Ask God to reveal the truth about Himself to you.

DAY 16: LOOK UP

It was a cold, grey April and spring couldn't come soon enough. Beneath wind-shivered maples, I wandered slump-shouldered across brown grass.

Illness and divorce had visited our family and financial strain and church family upheaval pulled my face into hard lines. Our two children were once again growing into another stage. It was time to step up my parenting, though I had no clue how.

I stopped near the ditch to glimpse the water. Edged by a thin line of green, dark water reflected grey clouds. I pulled the sweater tight around me as April air chilled me.

The snow had disappeared weeks ago, leaving behind flat brown blades and vacant branches. All seemed… grey. I felt old and spent and didn't know how to parent my kids anymore. Maybe I'd used up all my abilities. Perhaps my brain had finally disintegrated in the abyss of repeated parental instructions and the deaf ears on which they fell. With my eyes still fixed on the murky water, a sigh escaped. *"God, help me! I don't even know what to pray right now!"*

And there, beneath bare limbs, they came; the voiceless words. *"Look up"*

I raised my eyes, perhaps for the first time that day, and there, at eye level, a bright green bulb peeked from its branch, promising to emerge soon. A smile broadened as I was filled with hope.

I was not abandoned, to be forever surrounded by stark branches and the monochrome of in-between.

Spring always follows winter.

I left the oasis refreshed. By still water, the words of my Father restored my soul. It was the end of a grey season and a new one was birthing – one of vibrant colors, one brimming with new life.

*He lets me rest in green meadows; he leads me beside peaceful streams.
He renews my strength. He guides me along right paths, bringing honor to his name.
Even when I walk through the darkest valley, I will not be afraid,
for you are close beside me.*

Psalm 23: 2-4a

Response:

Is there a struggle or an area of your life you don't know how to pray for? Tell God that. He loves to hear from us, even when we don't know what to say. Thank Him for walking with you in the valleys, sitting with you in the ashes, and celebrating with you on those hilltops. Thank Him too, that spring always follows winter. Always.

17: DEFYING SOUL GRAVITY

One morning, I had the house to myself, so I nestle into a camping chair outside in the fog, clutching my mug of hot coffee and spent time with God. Birds trilled and twittered, a misty rain gently rippled the ditch water nearby… and then it happened; that glorious moment when God shows me something.

He drew my attention the giant, old Willows in our yard. Some leaned precariously toward the ground, others reached for the sky. The trunks that bent toward the ground provided cover for birds, amusement for climbing, and a great place for a tire swing … at least for now. As gravity continues to pull on it though, it will eventually fall down.

The trunks that grew straight, seeming to reach toward heaven, were strong. And they would remain strong. Gravity would not pull them down as long as they continued to point skyward.

Then, as He does, He brought scripture to mind.

> *"… Don't be dejected and sad, for the joy of the Lord is your strength!"*
>
> Nehemiah 8:10

When my thoughts are bent toward this world's stresses and misery, it pulls and weighs on my soul. When I 'fix my thoughts on what is good' though, (Phil 4:8) remembering what God has done, I am filled with praise and joy, and am strengthened.

> *You thrill me, Lord, with all you have done for me!*
> *I sing for joy because of what you have done.*
>
> Psalm 92:4

Response:

Fixing our thoughts on Jesus takes effort. Sometimes it takes a lot of effort. Especially when we're out of practice. Ask God for one habit you can develop to fix your mind on Him more each day. It might mean spending fifteen minutes in nature, just waiting to see what He reveals, or it might mean deliberately choosing gratitude instead of complaining. Whatever comes to mind, choose to implement one habit today.

18: THE SUNDAY MORNING TULIP MIRACLE

One Sunday morning, in preparation for the Sunday school song and story time, I collected props from my yard. To illustrate God's glorious creation, and how we can experience it with our five senses, I clipped twigs with leaf buds peeking. I snuck little green flower buds, snips of juniper and globe cedar, and collected rocks from the driveway. I looked at my handful and was disappointed that all I found was green or grey. I walked around the whole yard, searching for more, but nothing was blooming yet. I wished I could find just one flower to show the color God creates.

As soon as I thought it, I rounded a corner of the house. My jaw dropped and I gasped. There, right between the two shrubs I'd already clipped from, a single, dazzling tulip had bloomed. Just then. It hadn't been open before – I'd looked!

God had provided this flower for our class and I was amazed that He cared about such things. We could have done without it. I could have illustrated the point a different way - but God provided for even such a need as that.

It gets better. On the way to church, the tulip opened wider and bigger and was fully opened in time for our class! The flower and the story of my finding it were the perfect demonstration of how we can experience God through creation, and how He is active in and caring of our every day lives.

After church, we took the flower home to be a stunning centerpiece for our dinner table. Then the tulip closed! I put it in the sun, desperate to coax it to open again, but to no avail. It had made its appearance.

That morning my faith was refreshed by the reminder that God is active in my life every day - in my relationships, my heart, and even in my flower garden. I pray he continues to give me eyes to see it.

"What is the price of five sparrows—two copper coins? Yet God does not forget a single one of them. And the very hairs on your head are all numbered. So don't be afraid; you are more valuable to God than a whole flock of sparrows."

Luke 12:6-7

Response:

Ask God to remind you of a time when He answered a prayer. The size of the prayer doesn't matter – it could have been a request for a parking spot or a plea for healing. Recognize that it was God, the Almighty Creator, who heard you and was glad to participate in your life. Thank Him for his personal love and ask Him to open your eyes to see more of it every day.

19: FINDING ONE TRUE THING

With hands clutching a mug of sweet coffee, I pinched my eyes closed to hear the sound of the ocean in tree leaves. Wind swayed them like waves. I opened my eyes to return to the reality of neighbours, concrete, and hydro lines. Far above it all, wind pushed thick layers of grey cloud toward the single patch of blue sky that was left. I considered how it must look above the clouds – sunny, clear sky, it must be a perfect day up there. The patch of blue shrank and was swallowed by a sky of grey. All was cloudy and grey from where I sat, yet I knew the sky above had not changed. It was still blue, sunny, and clear – I just couldn't see it.

I understand Solomon's rants about how life is, in many ways, useless or unfair or impossible to understand. My feelings, views, and beliefs seem real and solid to me but are, in fact, full of deception. They change based on circumstance or as I gain new understanding. How, then, can I maintain any opinion, belief, or feeling when it may not be real or true? What can I rely on?

The only constant is our unchanging God. He is the same yesterday, today and forever. What I feel, believe, or understand won't ever change who He is or what His plans are for me. As I know God more and more, I become more confident of who I am and what my purpose is. I also become more assured that he is the one right thing.

He is true. He is good. He is alive and real. Sometimes I can't see him beyond my grey clouds of misunderstanding, but he's still there and is still the same. Of all the things I'll never know or understand, that is one thing I can know for sure. God is real and good and unchanging.

Jesus Christ is the same yesterday, today and forever.

Hebrews 13:8

The human heart is the most deceitful of all things, and desperately wicked. Who really knows how bad it is?

Jeremiah 17:9

Trust in the Lord with all your heart; do not depend on your own understanding. Seek his will in all you do, and he will show you which path to take.

Proverbs 3:5,6

Response:

Is there something you don't understand about God that's really gnawing on your soul? Talk to Him about it. Then ask Him to help you trust Him instead of leaning on your own understanding, opinions, or feelings.

20: GROWTH WHEN TRANSPLANTED

It had been a week since the tender tomato plants had been transplanted. They'd outgrown the initial seedling container, and now had ample room to grow even more. Every day I checked on them, eager to see them thicken or shoot up tall and strong.

To my disappointment, even after a week, not only were they not growing, but they were becoming weaker. Their tender stalks leaned as though they were too tired to stand anymore. Their thin green leaves curled and sagged. A couple of plants even leaned far over to the edge of the pot. In short, they looked tired, pitiful, and ruined.

But, despite appearances, growth was happening. It was all beyond sight though, at the roots. The tender young plants had been uprooted and suddenly placed in new soil. The change these plants endured had set their growth back, but only temporarily. Their work was intense and critical now, but had to do with roots, not leaves, and certainly not with the growth of fruit.

Likewise, we can struggle with setback when we are transplanted. When we change jobs, become parents, are struck with illness, lose a loved one to death, leave a ministry, retire, or any number of life-changing circumstances, we leave one soil and are planted in another.

When we find ourselves in a new and challenging circumstance, we want to do it well. We want to learn fast, adapt quickly, and flourish immediately. No one likes feeling like the new kid on the job all the time. Yet this is how being transplanted feels. Every day feels new, uncomfortable, and we're completely out of our element. It can be scary and we can easily begin to feel like we won't make it.

When I think of the tomato plants and their struggle in their new pot, I'm encouraged. It's okay to struggle and not have fully grown fruit in my life. It's okay to not know what to do or how to feel when my mom has cancer or when my friend dies or when relationships fall apart.

Confusion, fear, and doubt will come. My leaves will curl, my stem weaken, and I'll need to rest. But I don't need to worry about what that looks like to others or even how it looks to me. This is root-strengthening time.

It is in that confusion and exhaustion, my roots need to find their strength and life in Jesus who revives my soul. He is the one who restores, refreshes, renews, and even grows fruit in my life. Whatever soil I'm in, as long as my roots are reaching for Him, I will thrive where I'm planted and fruit will come.

> *He leads me beside still waters. He restores my soul.*
> *He leads me in paths of righteousness for his name's sake.*
> *Even though I walk through the valley of the shadow of death,*
> *I will fear no evil, for you are with me;*
> *your rod and your staff, they comfort me.*
>
> Psalm 23:2a-4

Response:

What new soil have you been transplanted to? Give yourself grace for the transition. It might not look pretty or feel good, and that's okay. Trust that God is still working in you and in your circumstance, and work to continue toward obedience even now. Let your roots grow deep in Him.

21: ON MAPLE SAP AND HUMAN EFFORT

We've harvested many litres of syrup from our sixteen Maple trees.

Most of them were a foot or less in diameter. One tree though, was two to three feet in diameter. It was old and enormous, which meant we could install several taps and harvest more sap from that one tree than any other.

Its grand trunk-like arms spread to shade our entire deck. Those limbs were heavy though, being a foot in diameter themselves, and seemed to hang lower each year.

One year wind storm finally snapped off the lowest limb that shaded our deck. The force of that heavy limb breaking off actually split the whole base of the tree in half! We were mortified that our most mature, most productive Maple that gave shade to our sun-exposed deck might now die.

Replacing the tree was not an option. It would take decades for it to become harvest-ready. Whatever we had for Maple trees was what we would ever harvest from this yard. Any tree lost was harvest lost forever.

So we did what we could to save it.

My husband got out a length of heavy chain and wrapped it around the trunk. He pulled it tighter and tighter, hoping it would pinch the tree enough to grow together again. Then we left it, and hoped for the best.

For a few years, it didn't look good. The leaves still came every spring but the split, exposed inside of the trunk was splintering as it dried in the sun. We were sure it would die, and there was nothing we could do about it. All the strength we applied would never heal a tree. We could not make a tree live or produce sap. Only God could do that.

There was nothing we could do about it.

How many times do we try this in our own lives?

We manipulate, pressure, or try to control the people and circumstances in our lives to get or keep things the way we think they should be. Maybe it looks like walking on eggshells and controlling information. Maybe it looks like withdrawing or becoming confrontational. It can even look like praying a lot, believing we can affect change if we just pray hard enough.

We wrap the chains of our effort around the people and circumstances in our lives, but the truth is, there is nothing we can do about it. We can't change others. We can't even change ourselves. This might not sound encouraging, but it is actually freeing.

We are weak, and it pleased God to arrange it this way.

It wasn't to wield His power over weaklings either. It was so we would learn to rely on him – to trust Him. If we were strong enough and smart enough, what would we think we need God for? We would go on with our lives forgetting all about the One who created us and gave us breath.

When we rely on Him though, His glory is made to shine through us. Suddenly it becomes obvious to us and others that God is the one doing these things in and through us that we clearly can't on our own.

> "If you need wisdom, ask our generous God, and he will give it to you.
> He will not rebuke you for asking."
>
> James 1:5

> "Each time He said, "My grace is all you need. My power works best in weakness."
> So now I am glad to boast about my weaknesses,
> so that the power of Christ can work through me."
>
> 2 Corinthians 12:9

Response:

Whatever you're struggling with right now, perhaps it's forgiveness, ministry, or a difficult relationship, I hope you're encouraged by this: you can't do it. But God can. Thank God that His grace is sufficient even now. Ask Him to reveal how His strength will shine through your weakness. (And then trust it will, even if you don't get to know how right now.)

22: HIS MERCIES ARE SURPRISING EVERY MORNING

Sitting on the deck steps one afternoon, I cracked open the Word to Psalm 107. Sunlight glinted off the pages and I waited for my eyes to adjust.

The stanzas repeated the tales of wanderers and homeless people who were lost. They cried out to God for help, and He helped them. Which made sense. I knew has a soft place in His heart for the poor, lost, and homeless.

The Psalm then described those who were "in darkness and deepest gloom, imprisoned in iron chains of misery." Why? Because "they rebelled against the words of God, scorning the counsel of the Most High." Their darkness and gloom was their own doing. They'd brought it on themselves.

I thought, *Well these guys are obviously going to get it.* I mean, I've read the Old Testament. This is where they get swallowed up by the earth or turned into salt or something. They brought judgment on themselves, and God's going to deliver. Their cries to God for help were too late and too little.

Do you know what happened when they cried out to God for help?

"He saved then from their distress. He led them from the darkness and deepest gloom; He snapped their chains."

These? He would save rebels and mockers whose pain was well deserved?

Does His mercy know no bounds??

Tears streamed down my face at the endless, humble love of our God. He is too good to us. Even when we spit in His face, mock, rebel, or hide from Him, He will still accept us if we ask.

That He would bend His knee to us – selfish, foolish wanderers and rebels, just because He wants too, is a humility I cannot fathom. If anyone could be proud and demanding, it's God. And He chooses to bend His knee to us like a kind dad.

Even after walking with Him all these years, His deep and genuine adoration for us blows my mind.

He protected me when I lived a dangerous lifestyle in a seedy area among dangerous people. Oh, the hundreds of things that could have gone badly! He's healed my fingertips when no doctor could. He rescued me from a dog ready to attack. He saved my sister's life. He gave me children despite Endometriosis. He freed me from addictions.

He's rescued me, saved me, protected, and provided for me. And all despite my rebellion. He has indeed cared for me in ways I don't deserve. His kindness wrecks me. All that's left to say is praise and thanks.

> "Let them praise the Lord for his great love and for the wonderful things He has done for them."
>
> Psalm 107: 15, 21, 31

Response:

What are some wonderful things God has done for you? List them. Remember them. What has God saved you from? Let His goodness and mercy toward you sink in and turn to praise and deep gratitude.

23: FAITH IN THE FOG

Our yard and garden sit on a small patch of land beside a large hayfield. One morning, our entire yard and the neighbor's field were covered in a giant moving mist of fog. As grey erased the neighbor's house and crawled over the garden and toward the house, I marvelled at how thick it was. It covered everything from sight and all we could see was grey.

The thickness of that fog reminds me of the grey cloud of grief and difficulty that seemed to have surrounded me in the last year or two. It seemed to grow thicker and thicker each month. I ached for it to dissipate. I worked to remember what hope feels like. Still, it hung. And I could do nothing about it.

I don't know about you, but when I'm in difficulty, caught in a cloud of doubt or fear, I don't always run to God. Like Adam and Eve, I hide instead. Because surely I have to fix it first. Fix me first.

But, of course, I *can't* fix it. Which means I can't yet approach God, which means I keep on hiding. The cloud thickens.

The glimmer of hope today is this: *I can't fix this.*

The bar is too high. The pierce of this pain is too intense. I can't hide and I can't change.

This is the end of the road. (Are you encouraged yet?)

Precisely where this road ends though, is where a new one begins.

Where I stop trusting myself is where I start to trust God.

If I can't fix this or free myself from the fog, there is only One who can. And finally my eyes turn away from self and turn toward Him. And I'm sprawled before Him, face down, offering all that I am, which is not much, but I'm too worn out to hide anymore.

Finally a shaft of light pierces the cloud and I can praise the One who *can* help me.

> *"Why am I discouraged?*
> *Why is my heart so sad?*
> *I will put my hope in God!*
> *I will praise him again—"* (Psalm 43:5)

> *"My Savior and my God! You are my King and my God.*
> *You command victories for Israel.*
>
> *Only by your power can we push back our enemies;*
> *only in your name can we trample our foes.*
> *I do not trust in my bow;*
> *I do not count on my sword to save me.*
> *You are the one who gives us victory over our enemies;*
> *you disgrace those who hate us.*
> *O God, we give glory to you all day long*
> *and constantly praise your name."* (Psalm 44:4-8)

Even when thick fog surrounds us, nearly blocking everything from view, we can praise Him anyway. Practice trusting Him anyway. And ask friends to join us in praying against the fog of oppression.

And, most of all, we can decidedly, intentionally, fiercely fix our eyes on Him, the Author and Perfector of our faith, who is good and able to guard what we have entrusted to Him until the day of His return.

> *And let us run with endurance the race God has set before us.*
> *We do this by keeping our eyes on Jesus, the champion*
> *who initiates and perfects our faith.*
>
> Hebrews 12:1,2

Response:

Are you hiding from God? Do you feel like you have to fix yourself before you approach Him?

He is a good and kind Father who loves you just as you are. He's waiting for you with open arms. Come to Him and be made new, freed from the cloud.

Maybe you're in a fog and are coming to Him, but the cloud isn't lifting and you're getting tired of aching for it to lift. He has not left you alone. Remember what He has done for you, and turn your heart to thanks and praise even here in the fog, enduring to the end, by His grace.

24: FRUIT IN ALL SEASONS

Sometimes I wish we lived by a lake or river so I could hear the gurgling of water every day. What is it about the sight and sound of water that's so attractive? People flock to resorts around the world, and compete fiercely for waterfront property. Even city parks are furnished with fountains for the relaxing experience of water.

I love the sound of water, but I'm a prairie girl surrounded by land, land, and more land. The oceans I see and hear are the sprawling wheat fields waving in the wind and the big blue sky with its whitecap clouds. Even here on the prairie though, the sound of rushing water can be heard in the flapping of leaves in the wind. A good breeze can make it sound like our little house on the prairie is surrounded by crashing waves.

I once read somewhere that the most pleasant sound to human ears is the sound of rushing water. It's interesting to consider then, that scripture describes God's voice as sounding like rushing water. There is comfort in it – or can be. Some might find it a reassuring sound, others might tremble with fear.

As followers of Jesus, we have a similar effect; we are able to emit a peace that comes only from Him. To some people it's unfamiliar and off-putting – something to be suspicious or afraid of. To others though, the peace is evident, attractive, and even translates into a comfort we can share.

"All praise to God, the Father of our Lord Jesus Christ. God is our merciful Father and the source of all comfort. He comforts us in all our troubles so that we can comfort others. When they are troubled, we will be able to give them the same comfort God has given us."

2 Corinthians 1:3,4

This fruit of peace and love – all the fruit of the Spirit - grows in us in all seasons.

But they delight in the law of the Lord, meditating on it day and night.

They are like trees planted along the riverbank, bearing fruit each season.

Their leaves never wither, and they prosper in all they do.

Psalm 1:2,3

But here's the challenge: the growth of that fruit doesn't always look the same in each season. And it especially doesn't feel the same.

I don't know about you, but I feel this pressure when trouble comes that I should be a shining example of faith. My face should glow like Stephen's did when he was pummeled with rocks. I should sing with joy as Paul and Silas did after their beatings and imprisonment. I should count it all joy, dear brothers and sisters, as James did.

At times praising God in the tough stuff feels easy and natural. Other times, it doesn't. And sometimes hanging onto faith in the struggle is a matter of grappling. Or hanging on. Or sitting in ashes and sackcloth, being still knowing He is God. It might not feel very faithful, but I am learning that it is. And God is gracious to the weak and struggling. Ours is simply to trust, even if we can only do it weakly for a time.

Even in times of trials and difficulty, we can experience and share Jesus' peace. We can draw from the Jesus' life-giving spring like trees planted along a riverbank and allow Him to produce His fruit in us.

Something that helps me trust Him when I feel anxious or worry that I'm failing is to meditate on this verse:

> "Don't worry about anything; instead, pray about everything. Tell God what you need, and thank him for all he has done. Then you will experience God's peace, which exceeds anything we can understand. His peace will guard your hearts and minds as you live in Christ Jesus."
>
> Philippians 4:6,7

This prescription for peace, when followed step by step, accomplishes exactly what it promises. When I do these things that fill me up with peace, (tell God what I need and thank Him for what He has done) I am refreshed and able to pass that peace on, even when I return to the same situation.

Feeling dry? Draw from the living water; He will produce fruit in you no matter the season.

Response: Whatever season you're in, trust that God is producing fruit in you. Even if you can't see it or don't feel it. Meditate on the above verses, reading them aloud. Choose to believe His promise that it is He who produces fruit in you.

25: WHEN IT FEELS LIKE NOTHING I DO MAKES A DIFFERENCE

Our family was gathered around the table with Mom and Dad to celebrate Easter. As we polished off the last of our dinner, conversation turned to gardening.

"How are your tomatoes doing?" Mom asked me. She had planted indoor tomatoes in January. Mine were planted in February.

"They're small and look weak. I hope they make it." Somehow, against all logic and reason, I always doubt the natural process of growth.

"Oh? How big are they?" Mom asked.

I raised my hands about eight inches apart. Mom's eyes widened.

"That's big! Ours are only a few inches tall!"

Days later, a friend came by to visit and also was impressed by the size of my tomato plants. I looked at them again. Maybe they really were doing well. How could I not see what they saw?

It felt a lot like when I left a ministry I'd been a part of for five years...

I looked back on all the seeds I'd sown over the years, and did not see any big growth. Sure, there were a few small changes that happened, but they were just little seedlings that would probably die anyway. There were no mature plants, and certainly not any visible fruit. What was there to show for my effort?

I was so deeply discouraged. I felt like I'd missed it. I'd obviously done it wrong and wasted my time and theirs. Ministry, I began to conclude, was obviously not for me.

What had I accomplished anyway?

And there it was; the whole cause of my discontent.

I wanted to know what *I* had done. Me.

Small wonder then, that I felt so discouraged and inept when I was looking to my own accomplishments for a sense of meaning or satisfaction.

The fact is I can't grow a single tomato.

The only thing I can do is plunk a seed in dirt.

I can't make anyone else grow spiritually either. I can't bring anyone to heaven or free anyone from sin or heartache. I can only sow seeds.I sow, God grows.

This discontentment with myself is probably exactly what I need. I need to let the idol of my own effort and good deeds die, and instead fix my affection on *God's* goodness.

And when I see what He has done – even if I think it looks weak and might die – I need to practice thanking Him. And trusting Him. And maybe, instead of assuming things will shrivel and die, I should even join His work by praying that His seedlings would flourish.

And then I need to walk away remembering that whether it grows or not is absolutely, completely, entirely His deal, not mine. He's got it. And He is able to keep what we entrust to Him.

And God chose me to be a preacher, an apostle, and a teacher of this Good News. That is why I am suffering here in prison. But I am not ashamed of it, for I know the one in whom I trust, and I am sure that he is able to guard what I have entrusted to him until the day of his return.

2 Timothy 1:11-12

Response:

Is there an area of life where you feel like your efforts are fruitless? Do you worry the investment you've made in others will result in little, or worse, nothing? Confess this doubt to Jesus. Ask Him to infuse you with hope and faith about that area by revealing How HE sees the situation. Then tell Him you will choose to trust Him with the seeds He's given you to sow, thankful for the chance to partner with Him in what He's doing.

ABOUT THE AUTHOR

Kimberly has been transformed by the living presence of Jesus, and strives to passionately follow and obey Him. She shares the faith-related insights with the aim of building up others in their faith and drawing them closer to Jesus.

She's currently working on the next book, *Parenting Meditations*, and *Surviving* (working title), the story of her journey through her mom's cancer.

Want a more inspiring inbox?

Visit Kim at www.KimberlyDawnRempel.com for more faith insights and to be in the know about upcoming projects.

Made in the USA
Columbia, SC
11 December 2023